D0883537

WITHDRAWN
FROM COLLECTION

# The Long Walk

*The Story of Navajo Captivity*

GREAT JOURNEYS

# The Long Walk

## *The Story of Navajo Captivity*

## *by Raymond Bial*

**BENCHMARK BOOKS**

MARSHALL CAVENDISH
NEW YORK

Benchmark Books
Marshall Cavendish
99 White Plains Road
Tarrytown, NY 10591-9001

© 2003 by Raymond Bial
Map copyright © 2003 by Marshall Cavendish Corporation
Map by Rodica Prato
All rights reserved. No part of this book may be reproduced in any form without written
permission of the publisher.

*Cover photograph*: This Navajo woman and her baby were captives at Bosque Redondo,
New Mexico, when this photograph was taken in 1866.

Photo Research by Candlepants Incorporated
Cover Photo: Museum of New Mexico #3242
The photographs in this book are used by permission and through the courtesy of:
*National Park Service*: 2–3; *Museum of New Mexico*: (#38194) 8, (#9833) 40, (#22938)
45, (#1816) 56, (#28532) 60, (#38206) 61, (#28534) 71, (#15949) 72; *Denver Public
Library, Western History Collection*: 10, 63; *Northern Arizona University, Cline Library*: 13,
14, 16, 18, 20, 22, 26, 28, 75, 77, 79; *General Research Library, New York Public Library.
Astor Lenox Tilden Foundation*: 30; *Amon Carter Museum, Fort Worth, Texas*: Rudolf D. L.
Cronau, Eine Strasse in Alt-Alberquerque, Nue Mexiko, 1885, collotype, accession
#1966.80: 32; *United States Military Academy*: 35; *National Archives*: 42, 69; *Arizona
Historical Society*: (#61569) 38–39; *Corbis*: Underwood & Underwood, 47; 54; Bettmann,
66 (top); *Smithsonian Institute*: 52, 66 (bottom); *Raymond Bial*: 82, 85, 87, 88.

Library of Congress Cataloging-in-Publication Data
Bial, Raymond.
The Long Walk : the story of Navajo captivity / by Raymond Bial.
p. cm. — (Great journeys)
Includes bibliographical references and index.
Summary: Presents an overview of the history of the Navajo Indians, with a detailed
account of how the United States government, represented by Kit Carson, forced them on
a 300-mile walk from their homeland in the Southwest to a prison camp at Bosque
Redondo, New Mexico, in 1864, and their eventual return home after the United States-
Navajo Treaty of 1868.
ISBN 0-7614-1322-7
1. Navajo Long Walk, 1863–1867—Juvenile literature. 2. Bosque Redondo Indian
Reservation (N.M.)—Juvenile literature. 3. Navajo Indians—History—Juvenile literature.
[1. Navajo Indians. 2. Indians of North America—Southwest, New. 3. Navajo Long Walk,
1863–1867. 4. United States—History—19th century. 5. Carson, Kit, 1809–1868.
6. Barboncito, 1820–1871. 7. Bosque Redondo Indian Reservation (N.M.).
8. Southwest, New.[ I. Title. II. Great journeys (Benchmark Books (Firm))

E99 .N3 B532    2002    979.1004'972—dc 21    2001043969

Printed in the United States of America

1 3 5 6 4 2

# Contents

# Also by Raymond Bial

*Building America* series

*Lifeways* series

*Mist over the Mountains: Appalachia and Its People*

*Portrait of a Farm Family*

*Amish Home*

*Corn Belt Harvest*

*From the Heart of the Country*

*The Strength of These Arms: Life in the Slave Quarters*

*The Underground Railroad*

*Where Lincoln Walked*

# Foreword

I see the Earth.
I am looking at her and smile
Because she makes me happy.
The Earth, looking back at me
Is smiling too.
May I walk happily
And lightly
Upon her.

—Navajo Song

FOR GENERATIONS, THE NAVAJO (PRONOUNCED NAH-vah-hoe) LIVED
on the dry lands of their homeland in the southwestern region of North

America. They raised sheep and cattle. They wove blankets. They planted corn. Through trade, and also warfare, they came into contact with the camps and villages of their neighbors—the Utes, Pueblos, and other native peoples. Over time, the Spanish and then the Mexicans moved into the region, and hostilities increased as competition for land and resources intensified. Later, when the United States expanded into the Southwest after the Mexican War, white settlers came into conflict with the Navajo. Soldiers and warriors also clashed as the Navajo fought to defend their homeland—and their way of life.

Raids and skirmishes went on for decades as government officials and army officers sought to resolve the bitter conflict. In 1863, General James H. Carleton, commander of the U.S. Army in New Mexico, thought there might be gold on Navajo land. Determined not only to conquer the Navajo but to drive them from their homeland, Carleton ordered them on a forced march to eastern New Mexico. The destination

*All of these Navajo men and women were held as prisoners at Bosque Redondo, New Mexico, around 1866.*

was a place called Bosque Redondo, which means "round grove of trees," where cottonwoods grew along the Pecos River. Bosque Redondo sounds like it would be pleasant, but the land was subject to drought and floods, and the water was unfit to drink. Formerly a trading post, Bosque Redondo became the site of the notorious Fort Sumner—a prison camp and scene of one of the most tragic episodes in American history.

In 1863, the United States government launched an all-out campaign to hunt down Native American men, women, and children. General Carleton placed Colonel Christopher (Kit) Carson, who had already become a legend on the Western frontier as a scout and trapper, in command of the troops. In what was to become a bloody and ruthless war, Carleton also directed Carson to kill all Mescalero Apache men, and to take the women and children into custody. Carson embarked on "scorched-earth" campaigns to force the Navajo and Mescalero Apache to surrender and submit to captivity at Bosque Redondo. The soldiers were ordered to kill any man who refused to give himself up.

Eventually about five hundred Apache and more than eight thousand Navajo were captured or starved into submission. They were forced to march three hundred miles, from what is now northeastern Arizona and northwestern New Mexico to Bosque Redondo. In Carleton's own words, Bosque Redondo was to serve as a "spacious tribal reformatory," where the army would be "kind to them" and "teach their children how to read and write, teach them the arts of peace, teach them the truths of Christianity." For the tribes, however, Bosque Redondo was no more than a desolate scrap of land without adequate food or shelter. Intended as a reservation "to tame the savages," the place was a prison camp. This is the story of the Navajo's fight to remain in their homeland, their suffering on the painful journey that became known as the Long Walk, and their desperate struggle to survive years of brutal and heartbreaking exile.

*To the Navajo, the land was sacred. They revered Canyon de Chelly, set in the very heart of their ancestral homeland.*

# One

# A People's Journey

LIKE OTHER NATIVE AMERICANS, THE NAVAJO ORIGINALLY JOURNEYED TO North America from Siberia, most likely crossing a narrow land bridge to what is now Alaska. For thousands of years they made their home in the Far North—in the Alaskan interior and the Canadian Rockies. They spoke the same Athapaskan language as many other tribes still living in this cool, forested land. Like their cousins the Apaches, the Navajo are linked by language and custom to native peoples who continue to hunt game and fish for salmon in the inland Northwest. To this very day they tell some of the same stories. Also, Navajo dwellings, which are called hogans (from the word *hooghan*, meaning "home"), may be based on the huts of supple willow branches covered with animal skins made by native peoples of inland Alaska and western Canada.

However, hundreds of years ago, between 1000 and 1500 A.D., the Navajo migrated into the highlands of the American Southwest. No one knows why the Navajo, after thousands of years in the cool, moist forests of the North, abandoned their homeland and moved so far south to the parched landscape of Arizona and New Mexico. In fact, the Navajo and the Apache are the only Athapaskan-speaking people in the thousands of miles of forests, mountains, and plains between the northern coast and the southern deserts.

It is believed that most of the Navajo journeyed southward in one burst of migration to the southwest, around Gobernador Canyon. Navajo origin stories place their emergence from the underworld there. Small groups of hunters—men, women, and children—followed over the next several generations. Later, as their way of life changed, the migrants drifted into two distinct groups: the wandering Apache, who continued to hunt, and the more settled Navajo, who learned to grow corn and other crops. Their name comes from the Spanish *Navajó*, which is derived from the Tewa Indian word *Navahu'*, meaning "large planted fields." Navajo and Apache people first encountered Spanish missionaries in the Black Mesa country of northern Arizona in 1626 and 1630. *Apachu* is most likely derived from the Zuni word for enemy. These native farmers were originally called *Apaches de Navahú*. Later, the name was shortened and slightly changed to Navajo. The Navajo call themselves Diné (din-NAY), which means "the People."

Hardy and clever, the Navajo crafted their weapons and tools from wood and stone, making whatever they needed for survival with their own hands. While the men hunted, the women and children gathered berries, nuts, and roots. The Navajo were also highly adaptable, and their ability to learn from other peoples became a distinctive feature of their way of life. From the time the Navajo arrived in the Southwest, they were strongly influenced by the Pueblo Indians. The two groups often engaged in peaceful trade. At other times Navajo warriors raided the Pueblo storehouses to steal corn, beans, and squash. They also kidnapped Pueblo women, who became their wives, and taught the Navajo new and useful

*The Navajo have long made their home in the Southwest, where ancient rivers have carved deep ravines into the rugged terrain.*

*The best known among the handicrafts of the Navajo are their blankets, painstakingly woven with intricate designs.*

skills, such as the cultivation of crops. The Navajo soon adopted many Pueblo customs and beliefs, including their origin story. They learned to weave, and they shed their animal-skin clothing in favor of cotton garments. They began to grow corn in the desert country of canyons and mesas between the Rio Grande and the Grand Canyon.

Although skilled hunters and gatherers, the Navajo gradually abandoned their nomadic way of life. When they encountered the Spanish in the early 1600s, they were already cultivating green fields of corn, weaving intricate baskets, and fashioning useful clay pots like the Pueblo. The Spanish taught the Navajo to raise domesticated livestock—horses, sheep, and cattle. By trading and raiding, they soon acquired their own animals. They became expert horsemen and herders of sheep and goats. From sheep came both meat and fluffy wool, which the Navajo wove into lovely blankets and rugs. Over the generations, weaving became integral to Navajo beliefs and their way of life. To this day, the Navajo are renowned for the complex and strikingly beautiful patterns.

*The Navajo often planted corn in the valleys where the shallow, meandering rivers provided a good source of water.*

# Two

# Sacred Land

FOR HUNDREDS OF YEARS, THE NAVAJO HAVE WALKED LIGHTLY UPON THE sandy soil of their homeland, which they reverently call *Dinetah*. The sacred land of the Navajo encompasses much of northeastern Arizona and western New Mexico, along with parts of Utah and Colorado. With millions of acres and relatively few people, it has long been a land of scattered bands that roamed over a landscape of many levels. Deep canyons that once sheltered cliff dwellers cut jaggedly through the landscape. In Canyon de Chelly, Arizona, for instance, the ruins of the Anasazi, or Ancient Ones, are hidden away on the rock ledges. At times, the Navajo also took shelter in these early dwellings. However, they most often lived in dome-shaped hogans scattered throughout the region.

In the soft, moist soil along the shallow rivers that wind through Canyon de Chelly, the Navajo tended their fields. They hunted and gathered, wandering the desert sands. They ranged over the tabletop mesas

*A lone horseman surveys the desert landscape, where there was little protection from the intense heat of the sun.*

that swept upward abruptly from the desert floor, and over the rose-colored sandstone of Monument Valley, sculpted by swirling winds over thousands of years. They journeyed through green sage and brittle grass flowing in the winds to plateaus dappled with piñon and juniper trees. They often ascended the slopes of surrounding mountains into high-country forests of pine and fir trees. From a distance, these ranges appeared to be streaked with pink, black, and white layers of shimmering rock.

The homeland of the Navajo is marked in each direction by the four sacred mountains: *Sis Naajini* (Blanca Peak) in the east; *Doo Ko' oosliid* (San Francisco Peak) in the west; *Tso dzilh* (Mount Taylor) in the south; and *Di-be Nitsaa'* (Hesperus Peak) in the north. Although the Navajo may not have been able to gaze upon every peak from their hogans, they knew they were blessed to live within the embrace of these mountains. To the Navajo, everything is alive, including the sun, rain, air, and earth—even the wind that sweeps over the land and comes out of one's mouth as breath. The Navajo deeply love the land through the days and seasons of their lives.

For hundreds of years, even after the arrival of the Spanish in the 1500s, the Navajo lived in hogans and other basic shelters. Families liked to live apart, far from any neighbors, and their homes were scattered among the rolling, sage-covered hills, the desert sands, and the rocky canyons. The next hogan or other sign of human life might be miles away—tucked beside a cliff or nestled among the pines. Small herds of sheep might graze in the distance, or horses may pick their way up a hillside. The Navajo long regarded their homeland as sacred—it was the Glittering World. Whether called the Three Sisters of Monument Valley, or Window Rock, or Rainbow Bridge, the land sustained the body and the soul. In the words of a Navajo prayer: "Beauty before me, beauty behind me, beauty above me, beauty beneath me."

Even when settlers and soldiers from the United States pushed into their territory, the Navajo never expected they would have to leave their

*Despite the hot, arid climate, the Navajo loved their homeland. Here, a boy lounges in the sand near his horse and sheep.*

beloved homeland, let alone be torn away against their will. However, new forces were sweeping over them like a dark and frightening shadow. For countless generations they had freely wandered over the land, until traders, then settlers, and finally soldiers began to appear on the horizon.

*Cooking pots simmer over the fire in the middle of this hogan, where two looms have been set up along the inside walls.*

# Three

# Navajo Home

HOGANS WERE REVERED AS HOMES AND PLACES OF WORSHIP, THEIR DESIGN ordained by the gods. Like the dome of the deep blue sky, the hogan's curved roof symbolized the universe. In Navajo belief, the original hogan was built by First Man and First Woman with poles of jewels: white shell, abalone, turquoise, and jet. However, this hogan was too small to hold all of the beings on Earth, so they expanded it by blowing on the poles. The hogan was then praised in song, along with its contents and the rainbow that arched overhead.

Early Navajo people lived in shelters with yucca or grass mat roofs. These basic homes had no doors, so people climbed a ladder to enter and exit through the smokehole. Other times, they occupied the abandoned cliff dwellings of the Anasazi. Later, the Navajo piled stones against cliff walls and lay poles overhead for a roof. For hundreds of years, however, they have preferred to live in hogans. Both the Pueblo and the Spanish

23

also influenced the hogan design. Styles have varied over time and by region. Three familiar types are the conical, forked-stick hogan; the dome-shaped hogan made of upright posts covered with earth; and the beehive hogan with horizontal logs laid in a hexagonal or octagonal pattern.

Forked-stick hogans were made of deadwood because the Navajo respected all living plants. They did not have axes to chop down trees, either. Although pine decays more quickly than juniper and piñon, it has a straight grain, and so it is most often used. Spruce, considered a sacred wood, was never used in making hogans. Builders leaned three posts together so the ends forked at the peak, creating a cone shape. The Navajo next laid smaller poles between these and then either plastered the structures with mud or left the wooden poles bare.

Similar to the forked-stick hogan, the dome-shaped hogan consisted of four upright posts around which other poles were laid. When mud or clay was applied to the outside, this hogan looked like an earthen mound. Builders always left a slightly off-center smokehole and a doorway facing east to receive the first light of each new day. Mats woven from yucca twine, grass, or juniper bark were hung over the doorway to keep out the wind and cold.

The Navajo also often constructed beehive hogans with six or eight sides. Logs were laid horizontally, slightly closer together from the bottom to the top of the roof, and plastered with mud to resemble an igloo. Over time, they came to build the walls higher. They threw soil on the roof to form a dome that deflected the hot sun and shed the occasional rain.

Consecrated in a special Blessing Way Ceremony to insure good fortune for those who lived within its walls, the finished hogan became a sacred place. Corn pollen, a symbol of fertility, was sprinkled on the dwelling as the medicine man, or chanter, offered a prayer for a long and happy life for its inhabitants. The hogan builders offered thanks to the white shell, turquoise, abalone, and jet—the materials they believed the first hogan was made from. Stone slabs, which outlasted wood, were sometimes set in the ground near the doorway in hopes of a long life for the hogan and its song.

One family usually lived in each hogan. Extended family members like grandparents, aunts, and uncles, lived there, too. People liked to situate their hogans well away from anyone else's home—the farther the better. Water, which was precious in the desert, was usually hauled from the nearest creek or spring. People also frequently had to travel great distances to gather firewood. Whether round, cone-shaped, or multi-sided, hogans had no windows or furniture, only sheepskin bedding, a few pots, clothes, and other belongings. The single door always faced east so that, upon waking, the inhabitants could greet the rising sun.

Because firewood was scarce it made sense, especially during the winter months, for people to share the warmth inside one hogan instead of living in many different homes. With many people in a small space, however, the Navajo had to treat each other with respect. They followed old customs, which assigned a proper place to each person and thing. Women always sat on the north side and men on the south. Children stayed near their mothers, and the place of honor for elders was on the west side, facing the doorway. Goods were either stacked against the walls or hung from the rafters. Cooking utensils were kept near the fire or stove. Along the west side they placed sheepskin bedrolls for visiting during the day, storytelling in the evening, and sleeping at night. Clothes were also usually stored in one place, and blankets—wrapped around the shoulders during the winter—were hung on horizontal poles.

The Navajo believe that ceremonial knowledge resided in the north, so people hung ritual herbs from the rafters and stored sacred minerals, as well as ceremonial belongings, in this part of the hogan. Tools to battle the evils of hunger and poverty, such as the man's hunting and silver-working equipment and the woman's grinding stones, were also kept here. Jewelry was quite valuable; it could be pawned, traded, or sold to keep away hunger, so it was hung on the wall, although often concealed

*Built in several different styles, hogans, such as this forked-stick hogan, provided shelter from the sun and wind.*

beneath clothing. Gambling and games of chance, which were considered powerful forms of knowledge, took place on the north side of the hogan. Through gambling one learned when to take risks, how to make the right decisions, and when to cease an activity altogether. Gambling was considered a discipline through which one learned responsible behavior.

Near the hogan, families built "shades," known to the Spanish as *ramadas*, which resembled porches with an open front. The Navajo constructed shades from four upright piñon corner posts to which they lashed horizontal crossbeams. They laid more poles on the top and sides, then covered the frame with juniper branches, leaving an open doorway that faced the rising sun. Traditionally, the hogan was the winter home. In the summer, people lived in the shade. The women cooked there and family members slept there, cooled by the evening breezes. They often dried corn on the roof because of good air circulation. Often, women set up their looms in the shade and wove blankets and rugs there, out of the heat of the sun.

The Navajo also built sweat lodges, or steam baths, near their hogans. Most often, sweat lodges were dug into the side of a hill, with doorways again facing east. Men heated stones in a fire, brought them into the sweat lodge, and sprinkled them with water to fill the lodge with steam. The steam opened the pores of their skin and was thought to purify their spirits. While in the sweat lodge, they chanted songs and invited the Holy People to join them. Invisible spirit beings, the Holy People served as spiritual guides. They taught the Navajo to be strengthened by the earth and to conduct themselves properly in everyday life.

The hogan usually had a sheep corral nearby. Because of sparse grazing areas, women and children herded sheep over large expanses of desert, but they penned the animals up at night. Along with their hardy breeds of sheep, most Navajo kept several Angora goats. These animals have large twisted horns and fine mohair, which is still highly prized by Navajo weavers.

*Made of upright posts covered with earth, this dome-shaped hogan was situated in the valley of Canyon de Chelly.*

When hunting, traveling, or setting up a sheep camp, the Navajo often built a temporary windbreak called a brush circle. These shelters were made by simply arranging dried branches in a circle. Sometimes, newly married couples lived in a brush circle while the mother stayed in the hogan nearby. Most often, newlyweds built a hogan near the home of the bride's mother. Over time, as daughters married, more hogans came to be clustered around the mother's home, like chicks around a hen.

This is how the Navajo made a home for themselves for hundreds of years, before and after the arrival of the Spanish and then the Americans.

# Four

# Shadows over the Land

WHEN THE SPANISH ARRIVED IN NORTH AMERICA, THEY BROUGHT MANY changes to the Navajo way of life. At first, the Spanish showed them how to ride horses and raise sheep. However, when missionaries attempted to force the Navajo to attend Catholic Mass, the Navajo simply moved away from the newcomers, whom they viewed as invaders. The Navajo were fiercely independent and were not willing to abandon their beliefs. Unfortunately, the neighboring Pueblos, who lived in villages and tended nearby fields, could not escape the Spanish, who soon enslaved them. Finally, after nearly a half-century of domination, the Pueblo rose up in 1680 and drove the Spanish out—all the way back toward Mexico. Many Navajo warriors joined in the Pueblo Revolt, and the people rejoiced at their liberation.

However, in 1692 the Spanish returned and again conquered the Pueblo and most of the native peoples of the Southwest—except the

*This street scene in Old Albuquerque, New Mexico, illustrates the strong influence of the Spanish throughout the Southwest.*

Apache and the Navajo, who deftly eluded Spanish soldiers. Through the second half of the eighteenth century, Spanish settlers began to move closer to the Navajo, into what is now northwestern New Mexico. The Navajo retaliated with raids, which forced many of the Spanish to abandon their ranches. The conflict went on for decades until, in 1786, Governor Juan Bautista of New Mexico concluded a treaty with the Navajo. Peace was generally kept for the remainder of the century. In the early 1800s, however, settlers again began to encroach on Navajo land. From 1821 to 1846, the Navajo and the Spanish engaged in another cycle of peace, broken treaties, and conflict. Attacks against the Spanish earned the Navajo a reputation as fierce warriors—just as Anglo settlers were pushing into the region.

After the Mexican War of 1846–1848, the United States took possession of the American Southwest, including the homeland of the Navajo. The Navajo now attacked the ranches and farms of Anglo settlers just as they had the Spanish settlements. Efforts to negotiate treaties failed, largely because the Navajo, with a population of about 12,000, lived in widely scattered bands. It was simply impossible to negotiate peace agreements with each and every one of these small groups. With no central tribal authority, each band acted independently and would not be bound by a single treaty. Many Navajo did take part in raids. However, it was mostly the United States that broke promises and violated truces. Government officials and the Navajo did not trust each other.

Anglo settlers and prospectors who ventured into New Mexico could have lived peacefully with the Navajo. Although renowned as warriors and raiders, the Navajo did not kill indiscriminately. However, the intruders were trying to take away their ancestral lands. The Navajo earned their reputation as great fighters mainly in defense of their own lands, property, and families. New Mexicans of both Spanish and Anglo descent often stole more than land and possessions. They kidnapped Navajo people, mostly women and children, and sold them into slavery. Moreover, the Navajo were required to return prisoners and livestock that they took in raids, while the New Mexicans who stole from them never had to. Captive native people were never returned—their families never saw them again. Several U.S. military leaders and Indian agents came to be sympathetic to the Navajo's struggle for survival. However, instead of a peaceful solution, a number of critical events led to even greater conflict and ultimately the removal of the Navajo.

On August 31, 1849, Colonel John Washington, along with James L. Calhoun, an Indian agent assigned to work with the Navajo, met in the Chuska Mountains with a Navajo band under the leadership of Chief Narbona and José Largo. The Navajo respected Narbona as one of their most distinguished chiefs. At the end of the meeting, a Mexican who had accompanied the soldiers declared that one of the Navajo men was riding a horse that had been stolen from him. Colonel Washington demanded that the Navajo surrender the horse to the Mexican. The Navajo denied the Mexican's claim and refused to give up the horse. As they turned to leave, Colonel Washington ordered his troops to fire on them. As the Navajo fled on horseback, the artillery opened fire. Seven Navajo men were killed, including Narbona, who was shot in the back. The killing of Narbona in such a shameful way fostered even greater mistrust among the Navajo. Narbona had always sought peaceful relations with the soldiers, only to be cut down. The Navajo lost all hope that the soldiers and settlers who were invading their homeland would treat them justly.

The Navajo were further angered in 1851 when the United States built Fort Defiance about thirty miles southeast of Canyon de Chelly—in the heart of Navajo territory—near what is now the city of Window Rock in northeastern Arizona. The government also established Fort Fauntleroy (later renamed Fort Wingate) in an effort to control the Navajo, but these military installations only caused greater resentment. Soldiers' horses now grazed on land that had long been grazed by Navajo sheep. As more settlers pushed into the region, they too began to graze large herds of sheep on Navajo lands.

On February 10, 1854, Major Henry L. Kendrick wrote to David Meriwether, governor of New Mexico, to protest the intrusion of these settlers. He explained that the disregard for native lands threatened his and Indian Agent Henry L. Dodge's efforts to foster peaceful relations with the Navajo. But the Bonneville Treaty of 1858 further reduced the amount of land recognized as belonging to the Navajo. To Kendrick, it made no sense to take away Navajo lands. Without good land on which they could graze sheep and grow corn, the Navajo would be forced to

*Major Henry L. Kendrick was one of the few U.S. soldiers to protest the encroachment of settlers into Navajo territory.*

become wards of the government or raiders. However, others sought not only grazing land but also gold, silver, and other minerals in the region, so they were eager to displace the Navajo.

The Navajo were occasionally able to deal with honest, competent, and fair-minded army and government officials, such as Major Kendrick and Agent Dodge. Indian agents like Dodge helped provide the Navajo with food and clothing. The efforts of these men led to times of peace and understanding. After he was appointed agent in 1853, Dodge lived with the Navajo and married a Navajo woman. However, in November 1856, while hunting deer south of Zuñi Pueblo, he was killed by a band of Apaches. Then, in 1857, Major Kendrick left Fort Defiance for a new assignment at West Point. In his place, Captain William T. H. Brooks, a hotheaded man who hated the Navajo, became the commanding officer at Fort Defiance. Brooks's appointment to this position ended any hope for peace between settlers in New Mexico territory and the Navajo.

Military officials disregarded all advice to seek peace, even from their own officers, and went ahead with a campaign to punish the Navajo. A cycle of bloody attacks and revenge killings ensued, culminating on the early morning of April 30, 1860, when about a thousand Navajo warriors attacked Fort Defiance under the leadership of the great chiefs, Manuelito and Barboncito. The Navajo were angered by the lack of justice and increased slave raids. Although most were armed only with bows and arrows, the Navajo nearly took the fort, but they were finally driven away. On July 30, 1860, the secretary of war ordered the army to embark on an intense military campaign against the Navajo. Troops slaughtered many people and captured others, burned crops, and slaughtered livestock across Navajo country. With the loss of their animals and crops, many Navajo faced starvation.

On February 15, 1861, Navajo leaders signed another peace agreement with Major Edward R. S. Canby, which included a government promise of rations for their people. The treaty acknowledged that the

Navajo had been victimized by deplorable slave raids. On February 27, Canby wrote to Army Department Commander T. T. Fauntleroy condemning the slave raids, which had continued even after the treaty was signed. He stated that he would "have no hesitation in treating as enemies of the United States any parties of Mexicans or Pueblo Indians who may be found in the country assigned to the Navajos."

On September 22, 1861, the Navajo went to Fort Fauntleroy, where supplies were handed out to them in a festive atmosphere that included horse races and enthusiastic betting. In the featured race, a thoroughbred owned by Finis Kavanaugh, the assistant surgeon at the post, competed against one of the finest Navajo horses. Both horses raced off to a fast start, but the Navajo horse could not be controlled and ran off the track within seconds. When the bridle was examined, it was discovered that the reins had been partly cut with a knife, causing them to break at the slightest pull. The Navajo had been tricked, but the race judges, all of whom were soldiers, declared Kavanaugh's horse to be the winner. The Navajo protested, shots were fired, and the troops retreated into the fort.

Colonel Manuel Chaves, the commander of the fort, was not sympathetic to the Navajo. In fact, earlier in his life, he had attacked the Navajo and kidnapped women and children as slaves. Chaves ordered the troops to open fire on the Navajo. He later falsely stated that the Navajo had tried to storm the fort. A follow-up investigation confirmed that only one drunken Navajo had attempted to get into the fort, and he was killed by a single shot from the sentry on duty. The soldiers began killing other Navajo people, despite the efforts of at least two sergeants to stop the massacre. Colonel Chaves also ordered his men to fire howitzers (small cannons) upon the defenseless Navajo. More than thirty people were killed, including many women and children. The wanton slaughter triggered another wave of violent revenge.

After this massacre, plans were begun in earnest for a major campaign to exile the Navajo to Fort Sumner (Bosque Redondo) in eastern

*This illustration by artist Joseph Heger depicts Fort Defiance in 1860 along with a cluster of hogans in the heart of Navajo country.*

*Colonel Manuel Chaves, the commander of Fort Fauntleroy, ordered his troops to open fire on the Navajo, and later falsely stated that the Navajo had attacked the fort.*

New Mexico, a place far from their homes. Here, the Navajo were to be "reformed." This is how Gloria Grant, years later, described the mistreatment of her people and the event that led up to the painful journey that came to be known as the Long Walk:

Raiding happened in order for us to survive. You know, they burned our fields, they killed our animals, they ran our sheep and horses off the cliffs. People to this day have never recovered. It's a very emotional topic for us. People starved, children starved, babies starved, and they took away our sources of food. They burned our peaches right here in the canyon where we lived. It was filled with orchards that have still never been restored. Raiding was not our way of life. We were forced to somehow feed our families.

But this isn't what the Long Walk was about. It wasn't about the itty-bitty raiding parties that went on. That was the façade they presented about us. It's all about natural resources; it has been and continues to be. We've got the land, they want it, and they'll do anything to get it.

*Barboncito became well known as a leader and eloquent speaker in defense of his people. He worked to establish the original Navajo Reservation in 1868.*

# Five

# Scorched Earth

Weary of Navajo raids on settlers in the territory of New Mexico, the U.S. government decided to end the strife by forcibly removing every Navajo man, woman, and child from his and her homeland. In the autumn of 1862, during the Civil War, General James H. Carleton became the new military commander for the territory of New Mexico. Arriving from California with a column of soldiers, he initially had three objectives: to defeat the Navajo, defend the territory from a Confederate attack, and establish a mail route in the region. However, after a long journey in which the troops did not encounter any Confederate forces, they were eager for combat. If they were not allowed to fight, the soldiers demanded that they be released from duty. So, Carleton organized an all-out campaign against the Navajo. He wanted to remove the Navajo not only for the sake of settlers, but also because he believed there was gold in the region. When the Navajo were gone, miners could dig for minerals in their sacred land. By 1863, the desire to find gold strongly influenced what should have been a strictly military decision to relocate the entire Navajo tribe.

As settlers and prospectors were threatened by unrelenting raids, Carleton, who was known for his ruthless handling of Indian raiders, became determined to subdue the Mescalero Apache and the Navajo. He intended to move them onto a distant reservation, where they would peacefully grow crops and raise livestock. Governor Henry Connelly and General Carleton agreed first to launch a war against the Apache and then subdue the Navajo. In 1863, Carleton directed Colonel Christopher "Kit" Carson to lead the troops in the field. Carson was not enthusiastic about the campaign because he believed that the Indians could be influenced to accept terms without bloodshed. He had also resigned as Indian agent to help protect New Mexico against the Confederates, not to fight the Apache or the Navajo. Yet, Carson had an abiding sense of loyalty to the United States so he reluctantly pursued the Mescalero Apache. In a campaign that lasted about five months, he defeated the approximately five hundred Apaches.

Meanwhile, Carleton had arranged for the Mescalero Apache to be relocated to Fort Sumner, the new military post that he had set up at Bosque Redondo on the Pecos River in east-central New Mexico. For nearly a century, Bosque Redondo had served as a trading post where the Spanish and then the Mexicans had bartered with the Apaches and the Comanches. Carleton had visited the region ten years earlier and believed it would be a good location for a reservation. However, because of the bad water, lack of firewood, and threat of floods, the board of officers recommended that he choose another site. Carleton ignored this advice and obtained President Abraham Lincoln's approval to set aside 13,000 acres to establish Fort Sumner on the river.

After the Apache were defeated and moved to Fort Sumner, Carleton and Carson turned their efforts against the Navajo. In April 1863,

*Brigadier General James H. Carleton, commander of the U.S. Army in New Mexico, strove to conquer the Navajo and drive them from their homeland.*

Carleton met with Navajo leaders who had remained peaceful and told them they would have to relocate to Bosque Redondo. This meeting was followed on June 15 with an order in which Carleton declared war on all the Navajo, including those who had never engaged in any conflict. On June 23, he ordered Lieutenant Colonel J. Francisco Chaves to meet with the peaceful Navajo again and "tell them they have until the twentieth day of July of this year to come in—they and all those who belong to what they call the peace party. That after that day every Navajoe [sic] that is seen will be considered as hostile, and treated accordingly." Meanwhile, Carleton was planning his campaign. He made no effort to communicate his ultimatum to the many bands scattered throughout the sprawling territory. Three weeks before the deadline, he ordered Carson to lead his troops into Navajo lands. Carson arrived at Fort Defiance on July 20, the day of the deadline, and embarked on a military campaign two days later.

Carleton devised a merciless approach to subduing the Navajo. On September 19, 1863, he wrote to Carson, "Say to them, 'Go to the Bosque Redondo, or we will pursue and destroy you. We will not make peace with you on any other terms. You have deceived us too often and robbed and murdered our people too long—to trust you again at large in your own country. This war will be pursued against you if it takes years...until you cease to exist or move'." Carleton claimed that Fort Sumner would be a "spacious tribal reformatory, away from the haunts and hills and hiding places of their country." In his view, the Navajo could be no more trusted than "the wolves that run through the mountains."

Red Shirt, as the Navajo called Carson, then rode to Canyon de Chelly in northeast Arizona and announced Carleton's order to the Navajo: "Surrender or die." He and his troops swept into Canyon de Chelly, terrorizing all who lived there. In a "scorched-earth" campaign, troops set fire to Navajo hogans and destroyed their food, clothing, and belongings. Soldiers also trampled fields of wheat and corn and slaughtered sheep and cattle. They polluted water holes. Carson also ordered his

*Colonel Christopher (Kit) Carson went to war against the Navajo and the Apache, yet he remained sympathetic to their plight.*

soldiers to chop down all the peach trees growing in the fertile bottom-land of Canyon de Chelly—between 1,000 and 1,200 trees. And the troops killed many people. Not only did the Navajo have to deal with the soldiers, but Ute and Pueblo Indians, as well as Mexicans, also attacked them and captured women and children to be sold as slaves.

The troops slaughtered people outright. By killing livestock and destroying food stores, they also left the Navajo vulnerable to starvation over the course of the ensuing winter. Families fled from the soldiers and tried to hide in caves in the canyon walls. They were hunted down and placed under arrest. In 1863, 301 Navajo were killed, 87 wounded, and 703 captured. Only 14 U.S. soldiers were killed and 21 wounded. Of the officers, 3 were killed, and 4 wounded. Within a few months, on January 6, 1864, Carson headed again for Canyon de Chelly, this time with 375 troops. Despite the bitter cold and deep snow, he returned with more than 200 prisoners. Carson treated the prisoners kindly, which was a major reason why many Navajo finally surrendered. They also told Carson that their people were starving and that many had already died. For many days they had lived only on berries and piñon nuts. The women were terrified that their children would be snatched away from them.

Through the rest of that hard winter, many Navajo straggled into U.S. Army forts. On February 26, 1864, Army troops escorted 1,445 Navajo men, women, and children from Los Pinos to Fort Sumner. In early March, over 2,500 Navajo people left Fort Canby for Fort Sumner (including those who had already died at Fort Canby). A total of 323 people died before reaching Fort Sumner. Along the way, New Mexicans stole Navajo livestock and captured those who couldn't keep up. Although these depredations are mentioned in army reports, no efforts were ever made to protect the people or to return captives to their loved ones.

Navajo men, women, and children were forced to walk the entire three hundred miles in this grueling journey that came to be known as the Long Walk. The route went east from their homeland, across New

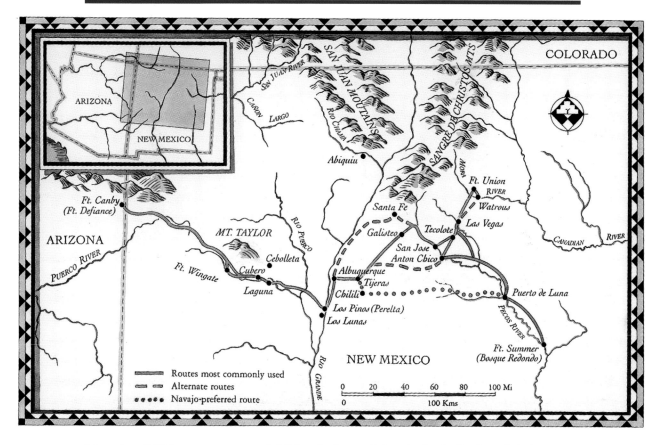

*More than 8,000 men, women, and children had to walk hundreds of miles from their homes to imprisonment. Many did not survive the journey.*

Mexico to Bosque Redondo. One Navajo person recalled, "According to my great-grandmother, when the journey to Fort Sumner began the Diné had hardly anything to comfort them or to keep them warm, like blankets. Women carried their babies on their backs and walked all the way hundreds of miles. They didn't know where they were headed." More than eight thousand people endured this forced march, often after being imprisoned for several months in the fort where they had surrendered.

Many fell ill and died along the way, and others collapsed after they arrived at the Bosque. The Navajo feared the worst because their religious beliefs had taught them never to cross three rivers—now they had forded the Rio Puerco, the Rio Grande, and the Rio Pecos on this sad journey. It was the first time in their history that the Navajo had been conquered and the first time they had ever been sent into exile. A small number of Navajo living in isolated locations in the west and north eluded the soldiers, but those bewildered people who were forced on the Long Walk suffered gravely. They didn't understand why they were being taken from their homeland and imprisoned—or even where they were going.

Author Tiana Bighorse described the forced march as follows:

The Long Walk is a tragic journey over frozen snow and rough rocks. There are a few wagons to haul some food and some things that belong to the white soldiers. The trip is on foot. People are shot down on the spot if they say they are tired or sick or if they stop to help someone. If a woman is in labor with a baby, she is killed. There is absolutely no mercy. Many get sick and get diarrhea because of the food. They are heartbroken because their families die on the way. Right outside Fort Defiance when the trip just starts, they sleep there and leave lots of bodies there. That's the way it is for the rest of the trip. There are bodies here and there and everywhere along the trail. About four thousand Navajos make the walk from Fort Defiance to Fort Sumner.

During this time of incredible hardship and sorrow, it was the elders and leaders who kept the people, many of whom were sick, injured, or exhausted, from giving up and laying down to die at the side of the trail. Tiana Bighorse described the actions of one great Navajo chief:

Barboncito is glad he is with the people, and some warriors that are with him are really a great help to the people. Barboncito doesn't get tired, and he just helps everyone on their feet so they don't get shot. Barboncito . . . gets the captain to agree to let the kids take turns riding on the wagon when they get tired . . . Some old men and old ladies, they have a hard time. Barboncito doesn't know how long it is going to take. He just has to keep the people going. He just has to keep giving them courage to keep on their feet. . . . Barboncito is glad when they get there so the people can rest, even if it is a terrible place to be. He is glad not to lose everybody.

Although at this time the Navajo numbered about 12,000, Carleton had estimated that there were only about 5,000. By February 1864, more than 3,000 had already surrendered, and he believed that the war was nearly over. However, many more Navajo men, women, and children surrendered to Kit Carson during his rampage through their homeland. A report by Captain Francis McCabe determined that, as of December 31, 1864, a total of 8,354 Navajo people were being held at Fort Sumner. By March 1865, the number had grown to 9,022 people. Afterward, until the Navajo were allowed to return to their homeland in 1868, the number steadily decreased. Many starved to death or succumbed to disease. Homesick and brokenhearted, others escaped.

Many Navajo did not make the Long Walk. They were captured and sold into slavery. Others hid in remote locations such as the Grand Canyon and Navajo Mountain. Some fled north of the San Juan and Colorado rivers to escape capture. A few even eluded the soldiers by daring to move into the territory of the Chiricahua Apache. One small band of Navajo from an area known as Kayenta discovered springs in a remote canyon behind the peak of Navajo Mountain. It is estimated that at least 1,000 to 2,000 Navajo managed to elude their pursuers here, sustained by the fresh water.

In a report to Washington, D.C., in February 1864, Kit Carson's bloody defeat of the Navajo at Canyon de Chelly was praised by General Carleton as the "crowning act" of Carson's long, distinguished career in

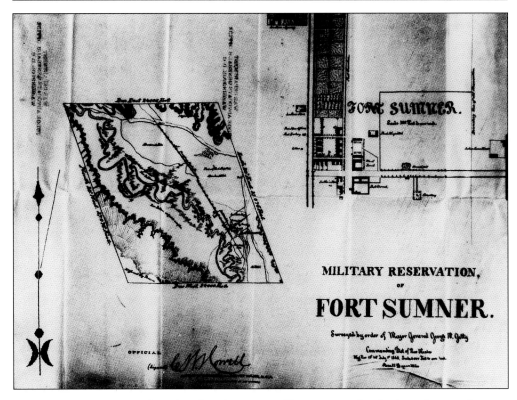

*In this map, Fort Sumner is aptly referred to as a "military reservation," where the Navajo were held against their will.*

"fighting the savages of the Rocky Mountains." However, to the Navajo, the brutal military campaign caused the destruction of homes, livestock, crops, and the deaths of thousands of people.

# Christopher Houston (Kit) Carson
## (1809–1868)

Even during his lifetime, Kit Carson was revered as a legend of the western frontier—a trapper, scout, soldier, and Indian fighter. He was born on Christmas Eve in 1809 in Madison County, Kentucky, and as a young boy he moved with his family to the little settlement of Boone's Lick, Missouri, where he spent most of his early childhood. His father died when he was only nine years old, and Carson went to work without ever receiving an education. He never learned to read or write. When he turned fourteen, Carson was apprenticed to a saddlemaker. A few years later, in 1826, he journeyed far from his Missouri home to Santa Fe, New Mexico, where he sought a new life.

Carson later moved to nearby Taos, New Mexico. From about 1828 to 1831, he made this mountain town his home base for fur-trapping expeditions that often took him as far away as California. Later, in the 1830s, he ventured through the Rocky Mountains and other parts of the West as a trapper. For a time in the early 1840s, he worked as a hunter for William Bent at Bent's Fort. During his wide-ranging travels, Carson lived among Indians and became quite familiar with native customs and languages. His first two wives were Indian—Arapaho and Cheyenne—respectively. Unlike many other trappers, however, Carson pursued a life of self-restraint and temperance. "Clean as a hound's tooth," recalled one acquaintance; a man whose "word was as sure as the sun

*Over the years, the legendary Kit Carson acquired a reputation for fierceness, though he was a mild-mannered man. This photograph shows Carson in his later years.*

coming up," related another. Carson became especially noted for his unassuming manner and quiet courage.

In 1842, while visiting his family back in Missouri, Carson happened to meet John C. Frémont, an explorer and soldier with strong political ambitions. Frémont soon hired Carson as a guide. Over the next several years, Carson led Frémont to Oregon and California and through much of the rugged terrain of the Rocky Mountains and the Great Basin. In his widely read reports, Frémont often praised Carson for his skills and intelligence in these expeditions, and he soon became a national hero. Carson was portrayed in popular fiction as a tough mountain man capable of heroic feats of skill and strength, even though he was a mild-mannered man of small stature.

Kit Carson's fame grew as he actively took part in several key events in the westward expansion of the United States. While serving as Frémont's guide, he joined the short-lived Bear Flag rebellion in California just before the outbreak of the Mexican-American War in 1846. Later that year, he also led U.S. forces under General Stephen Kearney from New Mexico into California when a band of Mexican soldiers challenged the American forces in Los Angeles. After the war, Carson returned to New Mexico and became a sheep rancher. In 1853, he and a partner drove a large flock of sheep to California. Boom times from the Gold Rush enabled them to realize a substantial profit from the sale of the sheep. That same year Carson was appointed federal Indian agent for northern New Mexico. He held this post until he assumed new duties in 1861 during the Civil War.

Carson played a prominent role during the Civil War. He helped to organize the New Mexico volunteer infantry, and saw action at Valverde in 1862. Most of his military efforts, however, were directed against the Navajo, who had been ordered by General Carleton to move to a distant reservation set up by the U.S. government. Beginning in 1863, Carson mounted a scorched-earth war against the Navajo. Marching through the heart of their territory, he destroyed their field crops, orchards, and livestock. Ute, Pueblo, Hopi and Zuni people, who had been at odds with the Navajo, took advantage of their old enemy's weakness by joining in the attack. Unable to defend themselves, most of the Navajo surrendered to Carson, who forced more than 8,000 men, women, and children to embark on the Long Walk. At the walk's end, the Navajo were confined until 1868, under terrible conditions of neglect and squalor.

Following his military campaign against the Navajo, Carson moved to Colorado to try to build his ranching enterprise. He died there in 1868—the same year the Navajo were allowed to return to their homeland. The following year his remains were moved to a small cemetery near his old home in Taos.

*Used as forced laborers while in captivity, Navajo men worked on a building at Fort Sumner.*

# Six

# At Bosque Redondo

When they talk about white soldiers being nice they're trivializing our experience. They're trivializing our history, and romanticizing it. They were real successful at hurting us, at removing us, at exterminating us. That's what the Long Walk was about, and they're just trying to pretty it up.

—Gloria Grant

GENERAL CARLETON RECEIVED LITTLE PRAISE AND MUCH CRITICISM FOR HIS actions in rounding up and imprisoning the Navajo. As military commander of New Mexico, Carleton declared martial law from 1861 to 1864, which prevented much public disagreement with his policies. But there was some. Two of his most vehement critics were Dr. Michael Steck, commissioner of Indian Affairs for New Mexico from 1863 to 1865, and Judge Joseph Knapp, a judge of the New Mexico Territorial Supreme Court assigned to govern from 1861 to 1864. Both men were eventually forced to resign their positions because of their opposition to Carleton.

Judge Knapp wrote to President Abraham Lincoln in 1864 to denounce Carleton for imprisoning the Navajo without trial or conviction, seizing their property without compensation, and setting up courts to try citizens for offenses for which there were no laws. In an open letter to Carleton published in February 1865 by the *Santa Fe New Mexican*, a newspaper that voiced opposition to Carleton, the judge contended that the general had never wanted peace with the Navajo. in another letter published in the newspaper on April 7, 1865, Knapp further asserted that Carleton had no authority to make war against the Apache and the Navajo. He reasoned that individual Navajo people were personally liable for illegal acts, but that Carleton could not punish the Navajo Nation as a whole. He wrote:

The peaceful Navajos, seeing Colonel Carson in their country, and trusting to his word and promises, also surrendered themselves, and you have taken them to the Bosque, as prisoners of war. Old men and women too decrepit to walk, little ones equally, yes more helpless, women and children, non combatants, and those not able to take care of themselves much less to fight, are all held as prisoners of war—persons who have voluntarily come in for their protection and food, are treated in the same manner as those taken with arms in their hands, if indeed, you have one such in your possession. Where do you find the rule for such conduct? Certainly not in any code of civilized warfare.

As early as December 10, 1863, Dr. Steck wrote to Commissioner of Indian Affairs William P. Dole regarding his opposition to detaining the Navajo at Bosque Redondo: "First, the arable land in the valley is not sufficient for both [Navajo and Mescalero Apache] tribes; and secondary, it would be difficult to manage two powerful tribes upon the same reservation." He further argued that it would be less costly for the government to support the Navajo in their homeland than at Bosque Redondo.

Unfortunately for the Navajo, the critics proved to be right. Government officials called it a reservation, but to the defeated and exiled Navajo, Bosque Redondo was a wretched prison camp. The barren land became the setting for a miserable ordeal for the Navajo—the worst tragedy in their history as a people. They lacked the most basic essentials—food, clothing, and shelter. Even the water from the Pecos River was unfit to drink, and caused severe intestinal problems. Moreover, when the Navajo arrived, they discovered that they would have to share the reservation with the Mescalero Apache. Although the Navajo and the Apaches were distant cousins, they had become enemies, and they no longer even spoke the same language. Fights soon broke out.

The Navajo had only the clothes on their backs—tattered wool dresses and deerhide shirts. The prisoners also had to make their own homes in the camp. They were given shovels, with which they dug holes in the ground. They placed tree branches over the holes to provide a little shade, and in these holes they lived. Occasionally they slaughtered cattle and used the hides as shades and windbreaks. There was scarcely any food, and people could not get used to the poor rations. Many got sick, especially children and old people. Everyone went hungry.

Howard Gorman, a Navajo who was imprisoned at Fort Sumner, told of conditions there in later years: "Some boys would wander off to where the mules and horses were corralled. There they would poke around in the manure to take undigested corn out of it. Then they would roast the corn in hot ashes to be eaten." The Navajo planted corn,

*The soldiers who guarded the prisoners at Fort Sumner slept in these barracks, while many Navajo lived in pits dug in the ground.*

pumpkins, beans, and wheat, but these crops failed every year from 1864 to 1867. The soil was simply too poor to grow crops. Blight and drought also ravaged the crops. Worms devoured their corn, as did the grasshoppers that descended on their fields.

The Navajo at Bosque Redondo shivered through the winter because there was scarcely any wood for fires. After the bushes and small trees had been cut and burned, people had to dig mesquite roots for firewood. In

*In 1866, these Navajo leaders met with U.S. soldiers about the ration tickets that captives used for food and supplies.*

the cold, wind, and rain, people became ill. Far from their home, weakened by disease and starvation, the Navajo plunged into despair. People wasted away, and many died. They began to ask themselves why they had been forced to come to this land of death. Most had never taken part in any raids. The Navajo had lived peacefully in their homeland for hundreds of years.

In 1865, the Apaches deserted Bosque Redondo and returned to their own country in the Sacramento Mountains. Longing to be free, the Navajo called upon the Holy People to liberate them. In 1865, an anonymous Navajo declared, "Cage the badger and he will try to break from his prison and regain his native hole. Chain the eagle to the ground—he will strive to gain his freedom, and though he fails, he will lift his head and look up at the sky which is home—and we want to return to our mountains and plains, where we used to plant corn, wheat and beans." However, the Navajo endured years of agonizing hardship before government officials gradually recognized the tragedy unfolding at Bosque Redondo.

The beginning of the end did not come until September 19, 1866, when the secretary of war relieved General Carleton as commander of the Department of New Mexico. Then, in January 1867, authority over the Navajo was moved from the army to the Bureau of Indian Affairs. An investigation of Bosque Redondo was finally undertaken, and on November 12, 1867, Lieutenant R. McDonald recommended in a report that the experiment at Bosque Redondo had been a failure and that the Navajo should be moved elsewhere. That same year a peace commission established by Congress condemned the mistreatment of the Navajo and other native peoples. On May 28, 1868, General William T. Sherman and Colonel Samuel F. Tappan were sent to Fort Sumner to negotiate a treaty with the Navajo.

Officials discussed the possibilities of relocating the Navajo to Texas or Indian Territory (present-day Oklahoma). However, in the treaty session, it became very clear that the Navajo desperately wished to return to

*Wrapped in a blanket, this Navajo warrior defiantly stares back at the camera with bow and arrows in hand.*

# Letter from an Officer at Bosque Redondo

Most official accounts of the Long Walk and years of hardship at Bosque Redondo gloss over the depth of suffering of the Navajo people. However, the following letter from an officer to his wife at least touches upon the failures of the experiment.

Fort Sumner, New Mexico,
February 26th, 1864.

My dear Wife:

It is now so long since I have heard from you, that I begin to think that you have quit writing. It is equally a long time since I have written to you, but I have travelled many a weary mile and passed many a cold, cheerless night, since I wrote you last.

I wrote to you last from Military post of Los Pinos, New Mexico,— well, on the 7th of the present month I left that post, with 44 men of my company, having in charge 243 Navajo Indians, 81 of whom were men, the balance were women and children; the Indians comprised all ages, from the old man or woman of a hundred years, to the sucking babe; some of them were taken prisoners during the late expedition of Col. Kit Carson, against that nation; their fathers or brothers having been killed in battle; others of them came into the Forts Wingate and Canby and gave themselves up as prisoners. I had 16 wagons each drawn by 8 mules, which required about 35 Mexican teamsters; so you see that with soldiers, Indians, Mexicans, etc., etc., I had quite a command, but it required a constant vigilance on my part to prevent them from rising, if they wished so to do— and murdering us; also to prevent them from escaping. I was ordered to bring them to this post, (Fort Sumner); it is situated on the Rio Pecos, and is about due east from Fort Craig,—you will find it readily on a large map.

As I said before, I left Los Pinos, which is a beautiful place, with my "outfit" and arrived here on the 22nd, being on the road 15 days, long weary days, most of time in the mountains, three ranges of which I crossed over—the total distance in that time was 242 miles. While in the mountains we experienced very cold weather and some of the time having no water, but what we obtained by melting snow, and part of the time, we had no wood either to keep us warm, or melt our snow,—everything must have an end; so we finally arrived here safely. I had fed the last of the Indian provisions the day before, and my company were quite out of provisions. Four of the Indians died and were buried on the road, so I got here with 239 of the Red Skins, they causing me very little trouble other than feeding such a large number every day.

My dear wife, this is a terrible place; it is intended to make it the final home of all the Indians in this country; there are about fifteen hundred here now,—Navajos and Apaches, and as many more are expected here during the next three months; there are five small companies, including mine, of soldiers here, and it requires our constant attention to look out for them, As fast as any Indians are taken in any part of the country, they are sent here. The Rio Pecos is a little stream winding through an immense plain, and the water is terrible, and it is all that can be had within 50 miles; it is full of alkali and operates on a person like castor oil,—take the water, heat it a little, and the more you wash yourself with common soap, the dirtier you will get. We are one and all looking very anxiously for the 16th of August, when we will be allowed to go to our homes. Captain Cremony is here with his company; he is in very good health.

The mail came in today, but brought no letters from you. I will write to you by the next mail. Give my respects to all. My warmest love to yourself and babies, and believe me to be ever

Your loving husband,
George.

In 1868, General William T. Sherman, along with Colonel Samuel F. Tappon, negotiated a treaty with the Navajo at Fort Sumner.

These chiefs gathered during the critically important negotiations regarding the future of the Navajo as a people.

their homeland. The great Navajo leader Barboncito served as eloquent spokesperson for his people, declaring, "I hope to God that you will not ask me to go to any other country except my own....We do not want to go to the right or left, but straight back to our own country."

# Key Navajo Leaders and Signers of the Treaty of 1868

**Armijo** (active mid–1800s) was a successful farmer and leader in Navajo conflicts with the U.S. Army from 1863 to 1866. Although he advocated peace between the Navajo and settlers, he became a staunch ally of Manuelito when hostilities broke out in the 1860s. When Armijo finally surrendered in April 1864, after a long struggle with soldiers, he and his followers were relocated along with other Navajo to Bosque Redondo in New Mexico.

**Barboncito** (1820–1871), born at Canyon de Chelly, in the heart of Navajo country, was a ceremonial singer, war chief in the Navajo War of 1863–1866, and head chief during the negotiations of the Treaty of 1868, which allowed the Navajo to return to their homeland. In 1846, during the Mexican War, he signed a treaty with Alexander W. Doniphan. In it he agreed that the Navajo would not fight against the United States. However, in April 1860, after an incident in which soldiers killed Navajo horses in a dispute about grazing lands around Fort Defiance, Barboncito joined Manuelito in an attack on the post. In 1863, when ordered to move to Bosque Redondo in eastern New Mexico, he and his brothers joined the Navajo leader Manuelito in rebellion.

In September 1864, Barboncito was captured at Canyon de Chelly by troops led by Kit Carson. He was forced to move to Bosque Redondo with other Navajo and Mescalero Apache. For several months he endured the atrocious living conditions, then he escaped with about five hundred followers in June 1865. He rejoined Manuelito but surrendered a second time in November 1866, leading twenty-one followers to Fort Wingate.

*This historic photograph depicts the signatures on the treaty that allowed the Navajo to finally return to their beloved homeland.*

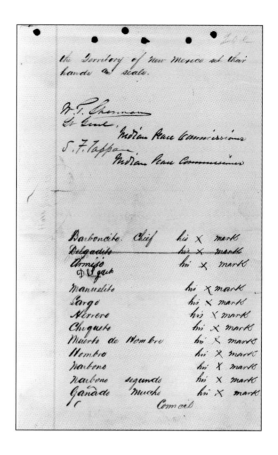

Barboncito became well known for his eloquent and passionate orations in defense of his people. His efforts were instrumental in establishing the original Navajo reservation in 1868 in the Chuska Mountains, where he died just three years later.

**Delgadito** (c. 1830–1870) was a medicine man and ceremonial singer who fought in the Navajo War of 1863–1866. He is also believed to have been the first silversmith among the Navajo. Around 1853, Delgadito made his first jewelry from silver coins. He taught jewelry-making to other Navajo artists, including his son Red Smith, thereby fostering what has become a prominent tradition among his people.

During conflicts with American troops, Delgadito and his brother Barboncito led five hundred warriors in alliance with Manuelito. In 1863, during Kit

Carson's scorched-earth campaign of destroying Navajo livestock and crops, the two brothers sought a peaceful solution. They agreed to settle near Fort Wingate, but they were forced to move to Bosque Redondo.

**Ganado Mucho** (c. 1809–1893), the son of a Navajo woman and a Hopi man, grew up to become a successful rancher near present-day Klagetoh, south of Canyon de Chelly in northeastern Arizona. He also became the leader of a band of Navajo people. In the 1850s, white settlers accused Ganado Mucho of stealing cattle because his herd was so large, but he and other Navajo ranchers signed an agreement to return any livestock that wandered into their herds.

During the Navajo War of 1863–1866, Ganado Mucho sought peace. When that was not possible, he and his followers eluded Kit Carson. Finally, in 1865, he led his band to Bosque Redondo to surrender there. He lost his son and two daughters to slave raids by Mexicans and Ute Indians. One of the signers of the Treaty of 1868 (allowing the Navajo to return to their ancestral homeland), Ganado Mucho rebuilt his herd and resumed his role as peacemaker between the Navajo and the settlers.

**Herrero Grande** (active mid–1800s) learned the craft of blacksmithing from George Carter while living at Fort Defiance in the 1850s. Just as Delgadito was esteemed for his silverwork, Herrero became well known for his knife blades, bits, and other bridle parts.

After a meeting with U.S. government officials at Fort Fauntleroy in 1861, Herrero was elected principal leader of the Navajo people. He resisted relocation and went into hiding. However, he finally surrendered in 1864, taking his band on the Long Walk to Bosque Redondo as ordered. He met with Manuelito on behalf of General James H. Carleton, but he was unable to convince him to surrender.

**Manuelito** (c. 1818–1894) rose to become a great warrior and married the daughter of war chief Narbona. During the winter of 1846, he skillfully eluded troops in Canyon de Chelly. Although Navajo leaders signed treaties that year and in 1849, he continued to defend Navajo ancestral lands. After the soldiers killed Navajo horses and warriors raided army herds, Manuelito was chosen leader. He continued the raids, and in retaliation the soldiers destroyed his home, crops, and livestock. In 1860, Manuelito led his forces against Fort

*During their long years of captivity at Fort Sumner, Navajo men, women, and children remained under armed guard.*

Defiance and nearly took the outpost. Colonel Edward Canby pursued him, but Manuelito and his warriors repelled the soldiers in a series of attacks. In 1861, Manuelito and other leaders agreed to work for peace, but raids and skirmishes continued. In 1863, Manuelito vigorously resisted encroachment on Navajo lands, even as Kit Carson embarked on a scorched-earth attack in which he destroyed Navajo homes, crops, and livestock. However, in November 1866, he finally appeared at Fort Wingate with twenty-three starving warriors. When the Navajo people returned to their homeland, Manuelito was named principal chief in 1870, as well as chief of police in 1872. He was succeeded in both positions by Henry Chee Dodge in 1885, after his retirement.

*Manuelito heroically defended Navajo territory, and when the Navajo returned to their homeland, he was named principal chief in 1870.*

# Seven

# Long Journey Home

ON JUNE 1, 1868, LARGELY THROUGH THE EFFORTS OF BARBONCITO, GOVernment officials finally entered into a treaty in which Navajo would be allowed to return to their home country, Dinetah. During their long captivity, the Navajo had lost about one-fourth of their people, and they were thrilled that they would soon be freed from the prison camp. It was reported that many of the old men and women cried with joy.

The deeply religious Navajo recall many stories that helped their cause in the treaty negotiations. Most often they speak of the Put the Bead in the Mouth ceremony. The people formed a circle around a coyote, which the Navajo have long revered as a sacred animal. Barboncito approached the coyote, which happened to be a female. The coyote faced east, in the direction of the rising sun, like the doorways of their hogans. The great leader caught the coyote and placed a bead, tapered at both ends and with a hole in the center, into the mouth of the animal. As he freed the coyote, she turned clockwise and walked to the west. Barboncito then announced, "There it is, we will be set free." Many Navajo continue to believe that this ceremony prompted their release from captivity.

At dawn on June 18, 1868, the Navajo at last started on the long journey home. A column of people ten miles long departed Fort Sumner. The contingent included 7,304 Navajo people, 1,500 horses and mules, and 2,000 sheep, along with 50 army wagons and an escort of 4 cavalry companies. One Navajo story recounts: "Children and food were put on the wagons. A great multitude journeyed over hill after hill, some on foot, some on horses, others in wagons. When they reached Fort Wingate, many were in a hurry and started taking off, saying, 'We are lonely for our beloved country. . . . '" In this poignant journey the Navajo trudged along dusty trails in the summer heat, not reaching their destination until the end of July. As they approached *Tso dzilh* (Mount Taylor), Manuelito later recalled, "We wondered if it was our mountain, and we felt like talking to the ground, we loved it so."

The Navajo could not imagine a fate worse than being torn from their homeland. They had long cherished their freedom and independence in their own country, within the embrace of the sacred mountains. Here, in this land given to them by the Holy People, they had led meaningful lives in which they provided for themselves. To be forced from this land and taken across three forbidding rivers had caused spiritual anguish as well as physical hardship. To this day, modern Navajo have bitter feelings about the forced march and the years of captivity, during which their ancestors were hungry and cold and often sick. In this hated place, many of their people had suffered. Many had died. The years at Bosque Redondo could have destroyed the Navajo as a people. Yet the Navajo are strong and they resisted all attempts to extinguish their way of life. Holding fast to their language and religion, they came joyously home. And there, on familiar ground, they devoted themselves to the long and arduous task of rebuilding their lives.

*When they were released from Bosque Redondo, many Navajo returned home and resumed their former way of life as shepherds.*

The brutal episode known as the Long Walk began to unite the Navajo as a people—for the first time in their history. Instead of viewing themselves as scattered bands, they gradually began to see themselves as a nation. Through the Treaty of 1868, they also possessed a sprawling reservation of 3,414,528 acres in New Mexico and Arizona. The Navajo believed that they were returning to their entire homeland as it was before their exile at Bosque Redondo. In reality, the reservation in northwestern New Mexico and northeastern Arizona encompassed only a small portion—no more than 10 percent—of the lands they had previously inhabited. As nonnative ranchers began to graze their sheep and cattle on ancestral lands not included in the reservation, conflicts arose.

After years of captivity, men, women, and children straggled back to Dinetah to face crushing poverty. Only five thousand sheep remained from the nearly half-million animals the Navajo had owned before the war with the United States. Yet at least the Navajo were home. Although the reservation was only a remnant of their former territory, the Navajo had not been permanently relocated to a strange land, unlike so many other native peoples. Moreover, the United States considered their land to have little economic value, so the Navajo were left in relative isolation.

Over time, they were able to steadily recover more of their territory. In 1878, an executive order returned 957,817 acres to the west side of the reservation. An executive order in 1880 added 996,403 acres to the east and south. Then, in 1882 and 1884, 2,373,870 acres were granted to the west and north. In 1900, the reservation was further increased by 1,575,369 acres. In 1901, the Navajo were awarded 425,171 acres on the southwest side, and in 1905, they received 67,000 acres in southeastern Utah. In 1907 and 1908, executive orders provided 1,208,486 more acres.

However, in 1911, lands in New Mexico were returned to the public domain. Between 1912 and 1917 minor changes were made to the boundaries of the reservation. In 1917 and 1918, the Navajo received 94,000 acres in Coconino County, Arizona. In 1930 and 1931, congressional acts gave the Navajo a total of 179,110 more acres. Then, in 1933, Congress granted them 552,000 acres in Utah. In 1934, small additions were made by act of Congress, and other minor changes were made in 1948, 1949, and 1958. Court decisions in 1962, 1963, and 1977 gave some disputed Navajo lands to the Hopi. Had the U.S. government

*Dotting the remote lands of the reservation, trading posts have long been a vital center of economic activity for the Navajo.*

known of the great wealth of minerals beneath the surface of the land, officials likely would not have allowed the reservation to grow to its present size.

Following their return from Bosque Redondo, the Navajo planted cornfields and tended to young trees in their peach orchards, and soon they were growing crops to feed themselves. They also worked hard and skillfully to restore their herds, gradually bringing the numbers of sheep, horses, and cattle back up to 1840s levels. They sent wool, hides, and meat to market. Women wove rugs and blankets and men crafted silver jewelry, which they sold at trading posts, and later to tourists. The Navajo soon became renowned as weavers and silversmiths, and they were able to command high prices for their work. The extra income helped ease their poverty.

With few towns in the region, trading posts became pivotal to Navajo survival from the 1870s to the present. Dotting the reservation, each of the trading posts was the economic center of its region. Traders were legendary characters—rugged yet keenly intelligent pioneers who generally treated the Navajo fairly. They lived with the Navajo and became members of the community. Traders helped resolve family and tribal problems. They wrote letters and filled out forms for people. The Navajo also loved the game of trading and respected those who made the best deal. People brought to the trading posts wool at shearing time and perhaps a few cattle at the annual fall roundup, along with stacks of hides, bags of piñon nuts, woven blankets, and handmade silver jewelry.

According to the terms of the Treaty of 1868, Navajo children had to attend school. The treaty stated, "In order to insure the civilization of the Indians entering into this treaty, the necessity of education is admitted." The U.S. government provided a teacher for every thirty children between the ages of six and sixteen. In 1869, a school was opened at Fort Defiance under the auspices of the Presbyterian Church. But the Navajo refused to send their students to the school, so it soon closed. The Navajo

*These two girls ride a horse through the desert as they tend their family's herd of sheep.*

opposed compulsory education, especially in boarding schools, because the children had to leave home and forsake their traditional way of life to attend. The Navajo believed that formal education would destroy their culture and identity. In 1893, Agent Dana L. Shipley tried to capture Navajo children and take them to Fort Defiance Boarding School. The Navajo resisted, and a man named Black Horse nearly killed the agent.

In the late 1800s, Christian missionaries were also moving onto the reservation, building schools and hospitals, and encouraging the Navajo to abandon their ancient beliefs. Few Navajo children attended either church-run or government schools. Those who did go often ended up running away from heavy-handed attempts to "civilize" them. In the early 1900s, more boarding schools were established in various areas of the reservation. The Navajo adamantly opposed having their children taken away from them. Some of the more distant schools located off the reservation were so far away that children were not even allowed to come home in the summer. Education was not only a threat to Navajo culture, but also a heartbreaking one, for many families were torn apart by it. The Navajo could deal with traders who merely exchanged goods, but they despised the educators and missionaries who wanted to obliterate their heritage.

In the 1930s, the Navajo suffered their most painful episode since the Long Walk. As early as 1894, government officials had reported that Navajo lands were possibly being overgrazed. In 1914, a priest at St. Michael's Mission again raised concerns that sheep and cattle were destroying the land. It was also noted that young children had to work long hours watching over the pasturing herds. In the late 1920s the federal government required herd reduction to ease the threat of soil erosion. Over the next few years, the Navajo were forced to slaughter or sell half their sheep. They were especially outraged when government officials left thousands of sheep to die in holding stalls. To this day, the Navajo bitterly dispute the need for herd reduction. It has taken a long time for their flocks to return to their former size. Sam Ahkeah, Navajo Tribal Council chair from 1946 to 1954, stated that livestock reduction was "the most devastating event in Navajo history since the imprisonment at Fort Sumner from 1864 to 1868."

*Today, many Navajo live in hogans with modern conveniences. This family home has a TV antenna and truck parked outside.*

# Eight

# The Navajo Today

THE NAVAJO STRAGGLED HOME FROM BOSQUE REDONDO WITH LITTLE more than the clothes on their backs. Yet, over time, they have not only recovered, but they have also grown as a nation. Since their return, their population has increased steadily. Today more than 300,000 people live on the reservation. The Navajo continue to honor traditional beliefs and practices, but they have also adapted to new ways. Although forced to attend boarding schools, they learned English and became familiar with the changing world around them. They adopted useful tools, such as metal plows and wagons. Highways and railroads were constructed around the reservation, and people began to drive automobiles and trucks. The federal government generally became more involved in the reservation, providing health care and doctors.

When the Navajo returned to their homeland, they did not have their own government. As before their exile, people simply scattered throughout the region, which remained under the authority of the government. The agent on the reservation appointed a head chief who was approved by the U.S. secretary of the interior. There were also a number of regional leaders scattered throughout the vast reservation—thirty in 1900. If a problem arose, the agent got in touch with the head chief, who summoned the regional chief to Fort Defiance. When the regional leader arrived, he discussed the matter with the head chief. There was little argument. Disobedience was strictly forbidden. The head chief was responsible directly to the agent, whose authority was enforced by the military at Fort Wingate.

In the early twentieth century, federal officials authorized the creation of five Navajo agencies. Dividing the reservation into regions added more bureaucracy and slowed the development of a central government, however. The Navajo did not establish their own official government until a half-century after the Long Walk. Even then, the government was formed only because speculators wanted to gain approval for mining leases on Navajo land. When oil was discovered on the reservation in 1921, it became clear to federal officials that the Navajo needed another form of government. The Midwest Refinery Company was allowed to negotiate with the San Juan Jurisdiction, where the oil had first been discovered. Initially, federal officials thought that the oil belonged to only the Navajo in that region. A council of Navajo living in that area was called and a lease of 4,800 acres was approved. Yet, as more of the reservation was laid open to mining, federal officials realized that the oil and gas belonged to everyone on the reservation. As other leases were sought, the Department of Interior developed a representative tribal government whose members came from all jurisdictions on the reservation. Gas and oil companies then had to deal with a central government under the leadership of the Navajo Tribal Council, which authorized all leases.

On January 27, 1923, Commissioner of Indian Affairs Charles H. Burke released a report called "Regulations Relating to the Navajo Tribe

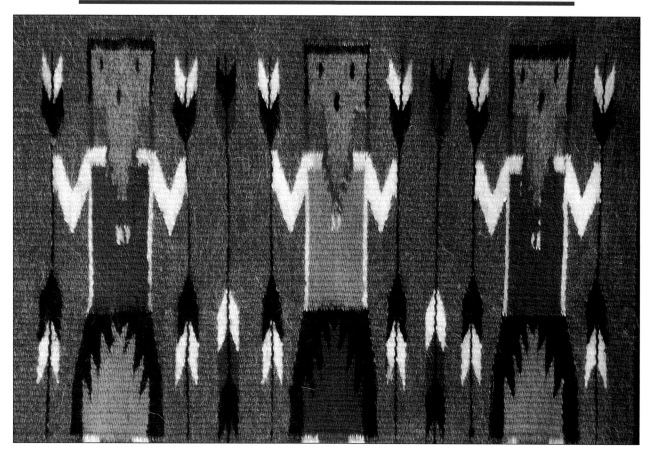

*To help support their families, many women weave blankets, which are highly valued by tourists and collectors.*

of Indians." Revised later that same year, the regulations provided for a commissioner of the Navajo Tribe to be appointed by the secretary of the interior. Steps were taken that year to also establish a tribal council with twelve delegates and twelve alternates. There were two delegates in each of the six existing jurisdictions—San Juan, Western Navajo, Southern Navajo, Pueblo Bonito, Leupp, and Moqui. The chairman was chosen from outside the membership of the council, and the vice chairman was selected by the delegates. The tribal council first met on July 7, 1923, at Toadlena, New Mexico. They approved gas and oil leases drawn up by the Bureau of Indian Affairs. The tribal council also granted authority to the commissioner of the Navajo tribe to approve all oil and gas leases on the reservation. Initially, tribal government was still closely managed by federal officials. However, over the years, the Navajo have fought for greater independence and control over their own destiny as a nation. By 1980 the tribal council was made up of more than 100 chapters.

Over the years, large deposits of coal and uranium have been found and exploited on the reservation. However, the discovery of mineral riches has been a mixed blessing for the Navajo. Emerging from an era of isolation, the Navajo have entered a controversial period. People living on the reservation hotly debate the mining and drilling that provides desperately needed capital for the impoverished Navajo but also ravages the sacred land of their ancestors.

Even as they struggle with poverty, the Navajo are sustained by their abiding love for their land, as expressed in the following song:

> In beauty I walk.
> With the pollen of dawn upon my path
> I wander.
> With beauty before me, I walk.
> With beauty behind me, I walk.
> On the trail of morning, I walk.

In 1968, a group of Navajo marked the hundredth anniversary of the Long Walk by returning to Fort Sumner to re-enact the signing of the peace treaty. They placed a marker near the Fort Sumner State Monument to commemorate the event, and to this very day they leave stones near the marker in memory of those who suffered on the Long Walk. That

*This woman works at her loom, which she has set up in the sunny yard outside her home on the reservation.*

*Navajo businesses, such as this roadside stand near Monument Valley, cater to the thousands of tourists who visit the reservation every year.*

year, part of the fort and the old Bosque Redondo Reservation were designated as a monument by the state of New Mexico.

Currently, plans are under way to build a memorial to the Navajo prisoners at Bosque Redondo. The state of New Mexico will construct a visitors center and exhibit at the site, and members of the Navajo Nation and the Mescalero Apache tribe will serve as project advisers. David Sloan, a Navajo architect living in Albuquerque, New Mexico, has been selected to design the center.

According to Gloria Grant,

They're always going to trivialize our history. To us, there are oral accounts of the Long Walk. They are things that happened, they are our stories. We still have to live with it today. White America just doesn't want to account for the atrocities that they committed against us. They don't want to understand—or teach their children—that we put our umbilical cords in this earth. This is our land, this is where we're from. And this is where we're staying.

# Bibliography

Arthur, Claudeen et al.. *Between Sacred Mountains: Navajo Stories and Lessons from the Land*. Tucson, AZ: Sun Tracks and the Univ. of Arizona Press, 1984.

Bailey, Lynn Robison. *Long Walk: A History of the Navajo Wars, 1846–1868*. Tucson, AZ: Westernlore Press, 1988.

Bighorse, Tiana. *Bighorse the Warrior*. Tucson, AZ: University of Arizona Press, 1990.

Erdoes, Richard. *Native Americans: The Navajos*. New York: Sterling Publishing Co., 1979.

Hooker, Kathy Eckles. *Time Among the Navajo: Traditional Lifeways on the Reserve*. Foreword by Danny K. Blackgoat. Santa Fe: Museum of New Mexico Press, 1991.

Iverson, Peter. *The Navajo Nation*. Albuquerque, NM: Univ. of New Mexico Press, 1981.

Johnson, Broderick H., ed. *Navajo Stories of the Long Walk Period*. Tsaile, AZ: Navajo Community College Press, 1970.

Kammer, Jerry. *The Second Long Walk: The Navajo-Hopi Land Dispute*. Albuquerque, NM: University of New Mexico Press, 1987.

Lassiter, Karl. *The Long Walk*. New York: Kensington Pub. Co., 1996.

Lindig, Wolfgang. *Navajo*. New York: Facts on File, 1993.

*Oral History Stories of the Long Walk = Hwéeldi Baa Hané*. Crownpoint, NM: Lake Valley Navajo School, 1991.

Ortiz, Alfonso. *Handbook of North American Indians: Southwest*. Washington, DC: Smithsonian Institution, 1983.

Redhouse, John. *The Forgotten Long Walk: When the Navajos Had Too Many People*. Albuquerque, NM: Redhouse/Wright Productions, 1986.

Trafzer, Clifford E. *Kit Carson Campaign: The Last Great Navajo War*. Norman: University of Oklahoma Press, 1982.

# Further Reading

The following books are recommended to young people who would like to learn more about the Long Walk and the Navajo people:

Armstrong, Nancy M. *Navajo Long Walk*. New York: Scholastic, 1996.

Bial, Raymond. *The Navajo*. Tarrytown, NY: Marshall Cavendish, 1999.

Bonvillain, Nancy. *The Navajos: People of the Southwest (Native Americans)*. Brookfield, CT: Millbrook Press, 1995.

Sneve, Virginia Driving Hawk. *The Navajos: A First Americans Book*. New York: Holiday House, 1993.

Stan, Susan. *The Navajo (Indian Tribes of America)*. Vero Beach, FL: Rourke Publications, 1989.

Wood, Leigh Hope. *The Navajo Indians*. New York: Chelsea House, 1991.

# Index

Page numbers for illustrations are in **boldface**.